THE AI REVOLUTION

THE AI REVOLUTION

NOLAN BLACKWOOD

CONTENTS

1. Introduction to Artificial Intelligence   1
2. The Impact of AI on Society   5
3. Preparing for the AI Revolution   11
4. AI in Business and Industry   17
5. AI in Healthcare   23
6. AI in Education   27
7. AI in Government and Public Services   31
8. AI and the Future of Work   37
9. The Ethical and Moral Dimensions of AI   41
10. AI and the Environment   45
11. The Future of AI Research and Development   49
12. Conclusion and Looking Ahead   55

Copyright © 2024 by Nolan Blackwood
All rights reserved. No part of this book may be reproduced in any manner whatsoever without written permission except in the case of brief quotations embodied in critical articles and reviews.
First Printing, 2024

CHAPTER 1

Introduction to Artificial Intelligence

We are on the cusp of a new era in which artificial intelligence has the potential to make greater, more inclusive prosperity a reality. What will define this era is our collective determination to harness advanced technologies, not to defeat one another in competition that will only leave the human race more vulnerable, but to make the very best of these tools in an inclusive, empowering, planet-friendly way.

Human-like robots, interactive virtual games, self-directing drones, self-driving cars, computer-based personal assistants, and business software are examples of hardware and software that rely on AI methods. Today, narrow AI is common and has been rapidly improving in recent years. Strong AI, also known as artificial general intelligence, is an AI system with generalized human cognitive abilities. When presented with an unfamiliar task, a strong AI system is capable of finding a solution without human intervention. Because AI is integrated and ultimately deployed in every industry, AI jobs are created in industries as diverse as healthcare, finance, and retail. Some researchers have called for fuller consideration of the potential of AI to create new intermediation, including new types of jobs in which newly educated workers help AI systems operate in value-generating tasks. Others have suggested that lifelong learning will be an essential attribute of a modern workforce.

Definition and History of AI

Some features related to AI history include an environment that seems to be dominated by favorable climate, together with unique people and informal relationships. Although resolute by the atomic fear controlled by the Cold War, AI origins can be traced back to the work developed either by Babbage more than 150 years ago or by the first electrical machines that would revolutionize the industry in the 19th century. In fact, the AI subject developed in parallel with the computing science when pioneers like Babbage showed the first giant calculator possessing what he called a brain.

The term "Artificial Intelligence" dates back to just over sixty years, while some tales related to its origins could be much older. The AI field is not an easy one to define. It can be considered as the established enterprise of asking computers to do things that people typically do better. A possible definition could be: Artificial Intelligence is the capability to learn, understand, and think. Machines proficient at achieving these capabilities are usually said to possess artificial intelligence (or AI). In any case, and the way the AI term is defined, some sort of abstraction plays the main role in comprehension and synthesis, abstraction being the main human axe offered.

Types of AI

However, it isn't likely that artificial general intelligence will be achieved in the next 50 years. Indeed, there is zero evidence that such a technology is either feasible or soon to come about - and indeed much evidence to the contrary. On the other hand, many types of artificial narrow intelligence are likely to be achieved in the coming years. Pony recognition by cameras, unethical computer hacking of our own emails and passwords, the ability to play games like chess and Go better than any human that has ever existed. Currently, almost every computer in the world already performs these superhuman MI-AI tasks. Even mobile phones with this superhuman artificial intelligence are present in more than 8 billion other intelligence devices and people everywhere.

If we're to talk about artificial intelligence and its impact, we first need to define what constitutes it. There are many types of possible artificial general intelligence, and these pertain to a general type of AI that can implement any and every cognitive skill just as a human being can. Indeed, if this type of artificial general intelligence could be achieved, it is quite likely that it would be more capable than human beings at these same cognitive skills. Subsequently, the more narrow types of artificial intelligence that we will discuss can be further categorized into two groups implementing technological systems capable of knowledge and skills that are either manual (artificial narrow intelligence - MM-AI) or mental (artificial narrow intelligence - MI-AI).

Applications of AI

First, the application of AI in many domains is often tenuous, and the organizations that are identified as AI leaders can also fund AI startups (providing a return on their investment). For AI to lead to significant job loss, there needs to be demand for a new set of tasks that AI can accomplish, and AI must be competitive relative to humans or other forms of automation. This does not always happen. For example, lots of startups, particularly those in Silicon Valley, have focused on self-driving cars. Yet there are significant regulatory, legal, and production problems that need to be solved before widespread use will occur. The same regulatory roadblocks that can prevent the widespread commercialization of AI-oriented products can also shape AI research. As a result, AI's connection to potential economic impacts is often assumed rather than exposed.

Second, successful innovation often requires a unity of science, engineering, and business. Yet there is often a disconnect between understanding of the AI technology and potential markets. Again, consider the billions of dollars being poured into self-driving cars. The amazing technical strides in computer vision and machine learning cannot be questioned, but it's simply not that clear if fully autonomous cars will be cheap and prevalent anytime soon. Not everyone has access to the new cars needed to make self-driving machine learning, rather than engineering, using car production capacity. And cars adjacent to the Capstone Project have not rushed to use high-quality, machine-learning tools.

CHAPTER 2

The Impact of AI on Society

So what does AI add to the mix? Just a few things. First, in addition to automation of previously overlooked areas, AI will also further amplify the capabilities of the already powerful areas of information technology. Today, those are big data, statistical analysis, and apparently all areas with a complex checklist. Secondly, since the efficiency-soaked sectors will gain disproportionately from adding special-purpose AI to the mix, all indications are that the industrial-automation-driven income-inequality trend we've been on will continue, getting amplified, unless new societal mechanisms are designed to cope with it. These will have to affect both production and distribution - to keep matters clear, I have not heard anyone suggest anything other than painful societal dislocation if uprooting turns out to be the only coping tool we can think of. Providing a universal basic income is a very nice idea, but distributing money does not directly address the real needs for society to get things done so that those relying on basic income still find society to be functional and also for more than the same price as today. Finally, thanks to machine learning, many of these boundaries are becoming statistically mighty foggy, making reliable predictions highly uncertain.

So, let's talk about all of these good and bad things that are going to come from AI. But I want to avoid the extremes that are being pushed on us through a media spectacle. Let me start by giving you a sense of how I approach the impact of a species-changing technology. The key is to understand that in the end, AI is no different than previous forms of automation; it's the most powerful form of automation we've ever had, but still, it's just automation. So to get a sense of AI's impact, I look at the roles that artificial intelligence can automate, which are the same roles that information technology has already been able to automate for the past several decades. Yet, you see that not all of these roles have been automated to the same extent; indeed, while some have been completely automated, there are some areas where humans have reigned supreme. I want to underscore that these fundamental challenges to the human condition are not due to biases in AI; they're very real effects, and the fact that they are finally being exposed is not a negative reflection of AI, but a sad commentary on the state of humanity.

Ethical Considerations

The second method for "second wave" AI generation – machine learning – arises from the tradition of cognitive science to a much larger extent than first wave AI. In machine learning, the learning algorithm is itself a piece of artificial intelligence that learns from the interactions of massive amounts of computational data. The creators of learning algorithms may seed their creations with initial values and objective functions, but thereafter the learning process is undirected. Ethical issues arising from this type of intelligence are not only different from traditional programming, but it also implicates a different group of relevant "programmers".

The first approach to "first wave" AI development is traditional computer programming. Expert computer coders write a program that dictates how the AI is to behave. The ethics of programming AI is simpler to enunciate – roughly, coders must avoid instructing the AI to carry out malevolent tasks. However, there are a number of issues underlying what is otherwise a clear directive.

The development of technology, such as AI, raises and heightens the stakes of ethical concerns. Two main forms of AI have recently emerged, based on two main distinctions as to how the intelligence is generated. These two approaches have different advantages and disadvantages, and enshrining an appropriate ethical code for the operation of each is paramount.

Economic Effects

At the same time, there is a grain of truth to fears and critiques about the rise of AI. This is especially the case if this time it is "different" with respect to all the other predictions of mass unemployment in the wake of rapid technological change. The observation holds if we understand that whether automation is about to substitute or about to complement workers depends on the ratio of productivity increase to the growth effect. Growth hitherto has often meant job creation as a strong side effect; as a result, even new classes of jobs emerge, and paradoxically, despite efficiency gains, labor and capital might increase, rather than decrease. The great unknowns come from the future effect of growth and neoliberal non-inclusive policy on these very productivity gains. The main takeaway from this subsection is thus that any debate on AI and its effect on labor must consider the distribution of power inside companies and the broader economy. The balance of power between shareholders, management, workers, and even customers within a company, and between the few and the many within the broader national or global economy, matters. And if what is happening is that the rewards of automation are diffracting to a lot of companies and/or individuals, this does not spell out much in general about what the outcome of this technological change will be.

When it comes to automation, the literature suggests that the balance ultimately shifts toward the income effect dominating the substitution effect. One relatively recent study from the United Kingdom, released in 2016, finds that the pattern has been that as more tasks have been automated, the more employment has grown. Jobs have not just been made in those industries adopting the new technologies; they have been created in accompanying industries as well. In the words of the authors of the study on labor demand within the United Kingdom: "The nineteenth century, through the introduction of the general purpose technologies in the second half of the twentieth century, the service economy, and service modernity, observed long run data is unable to find a negative effect of technology on jobs." Similar findings in the literature also argue that generally speaking, automation might not put people out of work, not even in the long term, because they will complement the new technology, as has historically been the case.

Legal and Regulatory Issues

The ground of safety and security is an essential target for AI development. The predictive quality of AI and machine learning functions like fraud detection and the like are used extensively now. Organizations are continuously scouting for the incoming innovations to help them solve problems and function more effectively. Because cybersecurity cyberattacks are rising drastically, it seems logical to have AI take on responses to improve system protection 24x7 in this respect, counterbalancing the rise in incursions. However, the question of whether AI can become more independent or autonomous in protecting us against cyber threats has arisen. Such an objective could be achieved by AI, calculated in milliseconds to respond faster than humans, guard against those problems, and improve defenses. The challenge for policy companies, politicians, the trade, and technology itself will be to introduce policies that shield us and exploit the benefits of AI.

To help master the legal and regulatory dynamics of artificial intelligence and profound change, virtually every jurisdiction is developing modifications. The pace of development is not across jurisdictions. Due to the urgent need to bring the regulatory framework up to date, international cooperation in such matters as data governance and in the drafting of industry standards, for example, will be very important. Set implementation rules and guidelines for the proper and secure development and operation of autonomous systems. The Ada Lovelace Institute, for example, recently launched an approach to help create these kinds of principles. It builds an understanding of the intersection of technology and ethics and contributes to the responsible and ethical adoption of AI. We hope that AI regulations evolve in a thoughtful way that secures our welfare as people, while at the same time promoting technology and growth.

CHAPTER 3

Preparing for the AI Revolution

Education systems should adapt to facilitate that skill. This is not a matter of merely forgoing more traditional education in favor of technical skills. In our model of T-level growth, those who combine complex communication with AI can, in some ways, be more valuable than those who do not. Those with both high productivity in complex communication and those who are capable of studying AI to the degree it affects their roles earn the highest wages. As AI shifts the frontier of what is economically possible, employers demand the linking of minds with the latest techniques. Indeed, the new AI-rich workplace needs to be characterized by a deeper division of labor between specialized workers and workplace generalists with the ability to work alongside increasingly sophisticated machines. Given the importance of jobs in the future, the fact that the skills required for many roles, particularly those involving high-level complex-matter problem solving, depend on both complex communication and the ability to work with AI is a cause for optimism. But realizing this potential is not guaranteed; how our educational systems adjust to the AI age will play a crucial role in determining how advantage of it we take.

Given the importance of the coming AI revolution, it is important to clarify which skills will be necessary to thrive. It is hard to predict what AI systems will be developed, but I argue that most roles humans could play in the future workplace will require them to both generate and work with complex information. These roles include research scientists, consultants, advertising and marketing specialists, engineers, and media, arts, and design workers. In short, complex communication emerges as the preeminent skill of the future workplace.

Upskilling and Reskilling

Countries will need to undertake far-reaching changes to their education and training systems to meet these challenges. Otherwise, millions of workers will be left over the coming years. Programs—both in traditional academic disciplines and around more vocational skills urgently need to be created. Moreover, we will need new tools to help individuals identify these career prospects, benchmark their skill sets against requirements, and enhance their capabilities. As long as a country is producing good-quality workers with advanced skills in these disciplines who can deliver performance productivity improvements in business and government, this should not be cause for concern. If anything, it would raise the growth potential simply by getting more of the current stock of leading-edge technologies implemented at a faster rate.

Upskilling is the acquisition of new skills to take on a new and better role; reskilling is the replacement of old skills with new skills as one's job changes. The most straightforward approach to career management is to become fluent in recent developments in AI, identify the challenges professionals will confront in adapting, and educate oneself on relevant skills. One approach to the identification of such trends comes from Erik Brynjolfsson, Daniel Rock, and Chad

Syverson at MIT. They have constructed a new measure of applied technical expertise utilization that overlays the content of over 5000 patents with over 20,000 occupation descriptions. They divide the economy into three major sectors: Jobs that use recent technologies intensively, jobs that use these technologies moderately, and jobs with little use of recent technologies. Workers in the first group earn about 10% more than workers with similar demographic characteristics (age, gender, race) in the second group, who in turn earn about 10% more than those in the third group.

Educational Initiatives

Society does acknowledge the shortcomings of standard educational models and channels resources toward valuable educational research leading to marginal gains. In addition, new paradigms have emerged. Some, driven by the phenomenon of "the flipped classroom," leverage the internet to both free the classroom from traditional, center-stage lecturing and to catalyze the spirit of communal learning, collaboration, and mentorship. The rise of Massive Open Online Courses (MOOCs) further unsettles traditional educational institutions and raises doubts about the very notion of charging students for information, compelling educators to focus on offering tangible value for society. Of course, simply making available online courses is not a panacea: designing and delivering quality online education by way of actionable and effective incentives is challenging and requires meticulous ongoing feedback analysis and careful policymaking. Even the mission of learning-at-your-pace can go awry, leading to exacerbation of divide already observed between learners with differing levels of socioeconomic status or between students perceiving education as meritocratic versus as a right. Underprivileged and politically silenced communities, college students, lifelong learners, and an aging population require different educational accommodation. An emerging challenge is how to replace institutional education as a prestigious form of selection for positions of power and prestige.

"Education is the most powerful weapon which you can use to change the world." – Changing the world clearly requires radical empowerment. Traditional educational systems have evolved little, reflecting fundamental limitations both in transferring knowledge and assessing its application. Encouragingly, however, insightful educational initiatives are continuously developing, striving toward both marginal improvement and the educationally revolutionary.

Adapting to Technological Change

Investing in education and research has long been observed to have high returns, in part because these investments lead to both growth through innovation and broader access to the demanding jobs these innovations create. The public investments in education and research will be a crucial tool for managing the shift in the impact of new technologies, and AI will make these policies even more effective. Where technological advance allows the marginal product of high-skill individuals to grow exponentially, investments that help spread these skills more broadly through the population become especially valuable. Given our deep and shared interest in ensuring that all Americans have the opportunity to make full use of their talents, the most important asset a nation has is its people, and it is worthwhile to bet heavily on the development of that asset, especially when there is data to suggest that smarter workers are the best formula for a higher income and for reducing income inequality.

Adaptation to technological change has brought significant challenges and real economic costs. The coming waves of more sophisticated AI will better capitalize on this reality because so much of the solution to harnessing this technology simply requires inventing things, which is something we do quite well. In the implementation stage, however, workers are not competing against machines but with machines, and history's most effective practice for raising the productivity of workers is to increase the skills of workers.

CHAPTER 4

AI in Business and Industry

Computer chips are now the most complex and compact things that humans have ever produced out of non-living matter. By becoming a partner of this new industrial giant, the microbial world has followed the strategies of humans and animals throughout history: investing symbiotic relationships. Microbes depend on chemical data from the economy of this tiny computer, communicate with it, and exchange information among themselves. With barely one percent of the genetic diversity required to carry out all of its functions, this economy is part of the human microbiome in charge of maintaining the harmony among its participants. This makes a human body a single cohesive existence. Although humans' behavior and personality develop from this harmony, the cosmos' complex construction follows very different rules to humankind's self-identity. These features unify the microbial world and the celestial world. However, as many have said before, Earth is only a very small part of the cosmos. Such an exciting discovery clarifies one of the main conundrums in planetary formation processes: the short timescales required for formation.

In the last chapter, I argued that AI capabilities form a critical part of a 'meta-innovation', which I define as the ability to automate the innovation process across as many of the stages of the gold standards of science, capital- or resource-intensive R&D, engineering, and manufacturing as possible. The countries, businesses, and organizations that optimally use and improve the AI capabilities on these four fronts will have a 'meta-competitive' advantage in the innovation race.

The transformational potential of AI in business is striking. The tens of millions of e-commerce customers of Amazon, the millions of advertisers on Google and Facebook, and the millions of freelance workers on specialized platforms like Uber, TaskRabbit, or 99designs already have some experiences of AI in sales, advertising, customer support, and hiring. But most other businesses are also keen to buy, customize, or assemble AI-enabled capabilities in their own domains. Although these will be mostly invisible to the general public, the business-to-business AI revolution is likely to be impressive over the next decade. Instead of continuing to perform clerical work behind the scenes, however, business AI is expected to move front and center, becoming the focus of business competition as much as marketing.

Automation and Efficiency

As models and methods improve, we can advance to statistical learning and deep learning with patterns and structured data. Machine learning models can improve and classify results for building, training, and punishing models that were developed for creating, validating, and deploying deep learning to improve models and generation of results. Tools that help describe inputs and outputs of cognitive AI. More complex tools aid generals in the effective application of multiple models to joint command AI. When significant network effects are present in a problem, we may also want to use moving agents for simulating the potential behavioral effects of different changes to the network or the agents within it for identity and role changes and additional ideas.

Progress in every industry should not only be seen in the products and services themselves, but in the processes and dynamics that allow those products and services to be created and delivered. The AI revolution is creating advancements in tools, products, and services to automate knowledge work, switching decision-making from humans to machines through rules-based models for applying known knowledge to inferences about new cases or decision trees to predict probable outcomes. In the simplest case, agents pre-calculate the highest-frequency inputs in a volumes context so they are known in the pre-consumer data point.

Data Analytics and Decision Making

BI tools have developed such that the technology is being used for more than branding and actually offers an enterprise-wide data warehouse that is positioned in the data center and is used for tactical and strategic decision-making. As described in Davenport, Harris, and Morison (2010), the change in business intelligence over the years has been the level of transparency, the range of skills required, and the impact the BI system has on corporate decision-making. Data analytics used in this manner makes a huge impact in the corporate world.

Data analytics is the science of examining raw data with the purpose of drawing conclusions about that information. Business intelligence (BI) uses data analytics tools to aid business managers in analyzing their own business data. There are many levels of business intelligence: the lowest level merely provides single-digit financial reporting, the highest level utilizes data mining to analyze all the data in question, according to given requests. Often BI applications use data gathered from a data warehouse or a data mart. Key performance indicators (KPI) help analysts identify potential problems, inefficiencies, and areas for improvement within the organization. It is important to note that while some tools may be used on a stand-alone basis, most utilize a variety of wide technologies.

Customer Experience

Ideally, spaceship Earth should become more like a luxury hotel with exceptional customer service rather than a creepy, covertly privacy-invading omniscient stranger. Any decisions or advice given to the customer should be accurate. During a live chat window either: bad translations, indecipherable text, style mismatches, or inarticulateness will seriously compromise the perceived intelligence of the conversing AI. Similarly, every day AI should be endeavoring to become ever more stylish, friendly and helpful in each mode of dialogue. When engagement fails to meet expectations, the customer may not be able to distinguish between the hairsplitting of an unreliable AI, the failure of a designer to anticipate a user's needs, or the incompetence of an organization to support its design.

Generally, the more technical, new, or unreliable a technology component is, the sooner an implementation will benefit from version 2.0 or from extensive research and piloting by early adopters. But in the case of customer facing technology, version 3.0 is too late. In the department stores of several decades ago, customers expected to mingle and chat while interacting with sales assistants who could offer fashion advice, customer-specific service, shopping companion support, and the handling of payments from wobbly infants through to senior citizens. Similarly, online, today's demanding customer expects access to these services at short notice, via computer, smartphone, voice-activated assistant, chatbot, and so on, without compromising on 24/7 availability and personal attention. Although there is no time like the present for a serious investment in customer experience support technologies, product selection and implementation should nevertheless be an informed and prudent one.

CHAPTER 5

AI in Healthcare

A friend of mine is a CEO at a large provider of primary and secondary care. He says AI is one of the only things he's seen in the thirteen years he's worked in healthcare that could be transformational. He's seen firsthand that AI, shaped by and applied to the world's largest healthcare dataset, is pushing the frontier of what's possible. The future is arriving. People concerned about their future healthcare costs, and all of us should be, should pay attention. Small probabilities can yield outsized benefits. The high variability and huge costs and benefits suggest that anyone with a healthcare exception should be asking themselves, how will healthcare benefit from AI and its plentiful data in the next few years? And what does that tell me to do today? It would seem that systemic reform is a probable practical result of some quantity of successful AI in healthcare. There are substantial changes coming.

Dr. Fei-Fei Li and I have written a paper on the use of AI technology in diagnosing and treating disease. Many people die from diseases that are preventable because they are not diagnosed early enough. The biggest culprits are cancers. But what if you could get an annual physical and just know for sure that you didn't have cancer? You still have to pay for the physical, but the quick painless confidence would be enormous. AI can and soon will be able to make it possible for many of us. Benefits of that sort are not limited to more effective prevention and treatment. They also include vastly improving the cost-effectiveness of the entire healthcare system.

Diagnosis and Treatment
Which brings us to the second, more fundamental reason why AI may usher in even greater disruptions than prior transformational technologies: the basic, core tasks of making almost any other technology or product that we could imagine today. The tasks that we currently use technology for are in fact far simpler and more specific than the capability of human intelligence in general, let alone what the statistical learning that underpins modern AI is getting close to. These tasks range from the biomolecular tasks of discovering drugs or mapping protein structure to the geopolitical tasks of espionage or cybersecurity to addressing the hardest material science and manufacturing challenges. Even relatively narrow AIs can automate nearly all information-based tasks of inventing technologies or products.

Like the introduction of machines into the workforce in the Industrial Revolution first and the introduction of low-wage foreign labor more recently, AI may increase overall wealth and output. Nonetheless, as in the Industrial Revolution, the creation of such wealth may either augment labor or largely transfer it from one group to another. The central reasons that AI will likely be so disruptive are twofold. First, because the intelligence of AI can scale so much more rapidly than through biological creation (the replication of humans, or bioengineering a more intelligent human), the timescale for such disruptions can oftentimes take the world by surprise. Economic history is littered with cases of transformational technologies that we could foresee from decades away, and other transformational technologies that took the world by surprise.

Personalized Medicine

But this is just the beginning. It is not just the DNA of humans that can be sequenced for relatively modest cost. The DNA of many different species can be sequenced, too, so that soon everyone's pet sheep will become a geneticist. New genetic material containing a gene for a favorable trait such as high muscle mass relative to fat could also be produced by rabbits or goats. Milk sounds good, with a gene that produces hornless bull's nature is lent on waing halters in payment for their allowed safeguards to their host animals emitted by GM yeasts designing therapeutics and vaccines, clothing, and biofuel-producing technologies.

Certain types of personalized medicine are partly to be expected. After all, everyone's DNA is different, so it stands to reason that everyone should have their own DNA mapped and analyzed in order to design drugs that work best in individuals. The first step in this direction has been taken: it is now possible to have your human DNA sequenced for a cost under a thousand dollars. In a few years, undoubtedly, every expectant parent will be deciding, prior to implantation, among a set of embryos created in vitro, and the DNA of those embryos will be sequenced and analyzed for a very large number of genetic diseases, non-disease conditions (referred to as normal traits or, in popular culture, "designer" traits), ancestry markers, etc.

Healthcare Administration

AI systems could compile a list of "common drugs on formulary that are predisposing our members to addictive or destructive behavior, increasing our service costs," and then increase or reduce utilization by combining connection efforts, information technology (IT) connections, and individual preference building, or stress physical space and nearby activities options. Similarly, given the complexity and importance of a first responder's work, an AI algorithm could provide on-the-spot advice on "practical" or "complex" tasks, reducing cases of non-compliance and system complexity. AI can also run EHRs on top of, giving real-time medical advice to health workers while they are performing their everyday duties, allowing them to share their opinions on different health outcomes for secondary products, reducing quality and costs.

Higher system usage, lower costs, and higher revenue opportunities could be generated by AI systems access programs that would orchestrate AI's different "bells and whistles" for people, logistical supplies, and physical spaces.

AI can improve payment models. Legislation to improve healthcare in the US has recently highlighted the importance of essential community providers in the healthcare support chain, making it easier for them to be adequately reimbursed for their work and therefore increasing the number of system users. These users are generally difficult to treat and can worsen hospital system financials. Another example is the difficulty in coordinating across different silos (outpatient, recovery, etc.) in the provision of certain complex treatments, such as organ transplants. AI systems could analyze data to build a more detailed and comprehensive list of transition steps, emphasizing their relative importance and degree of compliance to the customer (as a quality control) or the desired patient's ability to reduce relapse and associated costs.

Population aging is associated with a decreasing workforce and increasing demand for healthcare services. Over half of healthcare costs are related to healthcare administration, which is characterized by significant redundancies and information asymmetry among various players in the healthcare value chain. Opportunities for optimization through AI systems include improvements in payment models, system usage, coordination, compliance, and decision assistance.

CHAPTER 6

AI in Education

AI test grading has greatly improved over the last few years. As a result, some universities have started to use automatic grading for some of the multiple-choice questions on their exams. Such systems are able to provide students with immediate feedback. In the near future, they will be able to automatically grade student answers to simple questions posed in natural language. It is likely that within a few years university students will have to work on weekly tests that are machine graded in this way, with the aim of preparing the student for the final exam that tests the depth of understanding. This continuous grading will allow constant updating of the instruction process. It will factor in an individual's existing knowledge and progress step by step from simple problems to the current cutting edge.

We have already seen that AI is significantly enhancing (and will improve exponentially) electronic platforms for interactive online education. Augmented reality, virtual reality, online laboratories, gamified and customized instruction have started to be incorporated into course design and will increasingly do so. Work on intelligent tutoring systems has been progressing for a long time. These systems have the potential of interacting with students in natural language. Although they will not replace the major part of face-to-face educational interactions before AI has genuine understanding of natural language, they will be able to deal with some of the simpler learning needs of the students.

Personalized Learning

The roadmap toward AI-powered personalized learning includes several important directions at the intersections of pedagogy, scalable AI, and content understanding. We have encountered many of these directions before—whispers of their importance for engineering AI-driven platforms. They have now come together into an integrated roadmap. It's becoming clear why personalized instruction is crucial—both for class teaching and exclusively all online education programs. However, current approaches to personalized education can be expensive if the number of students is small and private education resources are required. This century, we are in the midst of a global rehaul of skills education, with more advanced learning management systems enhancing both the efficiency and benefits of online curriculums.

This century, we are developing more advanced personalized learning systems. These evolving systems' right content is more easily adaptable along multiple dimensions to a student's educational background, engagement, and learning pace. Recent results, in turn, are encouraging. Personalized learning already makes a difference for many students, and we are quietly advancing towards a future when it will not only offer a solution open to all the world's students but will also ensure that they too can explore their full potential and how they can help us.

Adaptive Assessments

This procedure is adaptive in two senses of the term. First, the program uses AI algorithms to tailor instruction to the particular needs of each student. If a student is struggling with a particular type of algebra problem, the AI software is immediately available to help. The extra time that a student needs to spend on the topic varies by student. Second, the software adapts to period-to-period fluctuation. If a student takes a month off during the holidays, the AI software knows how to get him back on track. Ensuring that students really do learn the material is a major concern in several physical education systems, so there is quite some excitement about the potential of having an adaptive AI-based testing system.

Our third area of potential impact is education. Artificial intelligence will usher in an era not of textbooks and rote repetition, but of the ability to interact with knowledge. Education will become more and more flexible. In 2006, Intellect Quest launched a commercial venture providing adaptive SAT coaching to high school students in the United States. This application may be simple, but it is instructive: rather than forcing students to work their way through a textbook, carrying out exercises in a standardized "unit" of time, students interact with Intellect Quest's AI-based software to help them learn all that they can.

Administrative Efficiency

Administrative efficiency: A clear target of AI is eliminating dull, repetitive labor in all its forms, ranging from washing dishes to digging ditches to filing W-2 forms. Technologically advanced products can endanger companies that don't keep up with them, to a point that such technologies are called "key disablers". Harmful new technologies are called "key enablers" by those wrongfully labeled as Luddites. Robotic administrative workers (suffering from none of the drawbacks and petty annoyances of the human variety) will take the place of the large fraction of human worker drones engaged in routine tasks in office settings all over the industrialized world. The same rule (AI is good at doing things that humans find mentally dull) applies to nearly any other organization.

CHAPTER 7

AI in Government and Public Services

Good examples of the kinds of government work that AI can help with are tax fraud, unemployment fraud, insurance fraud, credit card fraud, and other kinds of fraud in which people knowingly give incorrect information or make false claims. The basic ideas are to automate the enforcement of current rules or laws and to develop new rules incrementally to deny the fraudsters short-term gain from fraud. Using AI has the specific benefit of addressing the constantly changing forms of fraud, where people are constantly learning about ways to beat the system. Indeed, many organizations engaged in fraud detection find AI methods to be the only feasible work aides for developing complex schemes of rules. More advanced countries will use AI to help provide better services to more people. For example, they can immediately understand the instructions given by non-native speakers and provide content on request in multiple languages to enhance situational awareness.

AI will be used pervasively in government applications. In many cases, there are enormous benefits in terms of efficiency, error reduction, and cost savings for citizens. For example, AI is already used to detect fraud, waste, and abuse. Bringing greater efficiencies and cost savings to government will free up resources that can be used in ways that go beyond the institutional priorities of cost reduction. But using AI in government has the obvious and large social benefit that it can free up high-level state and city employees, who otherwise spend inordinate amounts of time mired in bureaucracy, to significantly raise the level of government service to their citizenry. These ideas about improving public sector organizations by using computerized work aides could be regularly updated to state current knowledge of cases of the use of AI to help government, such as those found on the AI websites of the federal government, the National Association of State Chief Information Officers, and the Center for Digital Government.

Smart Cities

The aim of the movement is to use data and technology to help design an urban environment that promotes a sense of community, reduces the need for car use, optimizes traffic flow, and supports well-being and health, among other goals. The foresight provided by technology, including AI and other advanced digital technologies like the Internet of Things (IoT), which connect embedded computers and devices to the internet, will create some of these capabilities. Already, AI engines can analyze and assess patterns in inputs of all kinds, enabling cities to forecast and respond to potential problems such as traffic build-ups, landfill repletion, and energy usage anomalies more effectively. The complexity of these technologies is rising. As the large body of literature in this field shows, there is no single model of what makes a city intelligent and what kind of intelligence is relevant for the purpose at hand. Many elements contribute to 'smart city' tool development.

The automation offered by AI is increasingly present across the economy and society. It enables a range of products, services, and business models that were not possible previously. 'Smart cities' are a prime example of this, as they profoundly change how we organize the urban environment and are becoming increasingly sophisticated. They have been around for a long time, with some elements of the original 'smart cities' dating back to ancient Greece. Historically, these planning features - of which the largest is often understood to be the sewage system - were often constructed to maintain public order and respond to hardships associated with high population density and reduced access to natural resources due to rising pollution levels. In the twenty-first century, smart cities reflect an application of advanced knowledge and technology to improve urban settlement.

Public Safety

A gradually shaped public attitude serves as a second line of defense: as ASI capability nears human level, an effort should be made to strengthen global norms aimed at remaining the boss. With a partial ascent, the incentive is for AI leaders to cooperate on global rules of the road. The goal is to create a high-level organizational firewall against engineered malevolence. If global norms become stronger, the world as a whole will be more secure, even if the likelihood of a bad outcome given a norm violation remains unacceptably high. The current dynamic is quite different; in the military sphere, the major powers are applying a technology-first, norms-later approach, while Chinese doctrine includes crowd control at home and deciding when war and military conflict should occur. We are headed for a dangerous unstable period. Some have called for banning fully autonomous systems to prevent the AI Armageddon, but it seems less likely that, since treaties against bioweapons do not seem to have a very high level of compliance with their norms. Another approach is to target decision-making entities of all types, hence the emphasis on gradual ascent, industry leadership, and the role model effect. That is why there could be meaningful transparency into intelligence organization thinking to help create a stable norm. For example, the strongest argument against inflicting suffering—an AI social melancholy would behave as a doomsday machine—relies on widespread public understanding of ASI's impact on happiness, on world media acting as a reliable interpreter.

Of paramount importance is preventing an ASI from having power in the physical world. In AI, there is already an unwritten rule that it is reckless to design AI systems that operate without a human in the loop. It is important to make this rule more explicit and more robust to make it difficult for this rule to be bypassed. The particular challenge with ASI is the risk that it will persuade humans to give it unchecked authority. The first line of defense is to apply the government principle: no single ASI—nor any inner group of ASIs—should have general executive authority. The structural principle outlined above helps ensure sectors of the economy are operated to safeguard the public good, but there may well be an AI-beneficent role just as there is a human-beneficent role in civil-military relations. For example, there would always be a need for technical advisors offered to decision-makers in every organization, including parts of government and the military. These new institutions should be designed not to duplicate traditional engineering functions but to complement them by advising on safety, fairness, and other social and ethical considerations.

Policy Making

Once we have agreed on the type of minimum capabilities that should not be so unevenly distributed but more equally shared, these can be provided by the public sector or through other participatory forms of governance, readiness or resilience. It is then appropriate to ensure that no private party uses technological tools, including AI, to mold people and influence opinions in such a way that private interests prevail over the public interest that is providing for those capabilities, how much less is acceptable. There is a need to be mindful of technology's potentially insidious agreements that differ disturbingly from what human beings would accomplish on their own, without mind control. These are capabilities and public control thereof that are simply not tolerated in our democracies. With AI we are challenged to make sure of that once more.

We have seen that regulation is more powerful and can be less arbitrary when it takes the form of a duty on those with more power vis-à-vis AI. This suggests that overall AI policy should give some special attention to the responsibilities that tend to come with the most capabilities. It should safeguard people from the misuse and abuse of AI and other technologies by concentrated power – be it in the public or the private sector. One way to describe what is very deep and powerful in the work on sufficiency economy is the idea of primitive accumulation of capabilities at the top end of the wealth distribution.

CHAPTER 8

AI and the Future of Work

In mid-2013, upon John Kelly's return to IBM's corporate labs after his decade-long stint as the senior vice president of IBM's Watson Group, he and a small number of his lab colleagues set out to estimate the impact of cognitive technologies, now also called AI, on the future of work. The goal was to gain a business advantage by modeling the range of technology-enabled tasks that employees would use to either remain competitive in an AI economy or achieve more value to counter anticipated wage stagnation and even job loss in the absence of additional investments in education.

But we foresaw another major cognitive era milestone growing out of another project, dubbed the Elevator Pitch Test. The essence of the test was to predict the AI moment that would signal the arrival of human-level AI. In other words, what was Watson's Jeopardy! win moment—the moment when AI surpasses human performance and becomes a competitor rather than a collaborator? Only about 5 percent of such economists expect AI will eliminate their own jobs, even as they expect AI and cognitive technologies will become increasingly relevant in the years ahead.

Online job postings provide a striking additional indicator of how much companies expect the competitive balance to shift—job postings show a greater preference for the more modestly skilled jobs that are harder to automate. But this survey also reveals AI-cognitive technology's potential impact on a much wider array of tasks, functions, and jobs than in prior surveys. Tasks involving physical skill, emotional response, and human interaction can also be automated, but they generally fall into the category of things that we want—but our machines don't yet provide—the outstanding levels of subjective personal experiences instead of objective functionality that we seek to generate value.

Job Displacement and Creation

Like the invention of the steam engine, the automobile and the computer, the invention of AI is a revolution that will change fundamental aspects of societies. Distinctly from previous industrial revolutions that were localized in certain sectors, while creating more opportunities than they destroyed, AI will have a profound impact on the world of work. Depending on forecast methodology, estimates of possible job loss due to the introduction of AI in the economy are high and worrisome. If we let it be, AI will only increase the ratio of capital to labor, causing the already increasing gap in income distribution among people to increase even more. These are real risks, and the whole society will be regulated according to the path we are going to take into the AI revolution.

We are going through a period of great upheaval at present. Upheavals are like partly filled, upturned bottles of water. When they happen, the liquid is sloshing all over the place. Times of difficulty, however, need not be times of despair. AI is creating new opportunities in every discipline. We have the privilege of living through what promises to be the most important period in history. Imagine the time one might have wanted to live: the age of Leonardo in science, the age of Pericles in politics, the age of Beethoven in music. Now think of the people of 2100 thinking of us. There is nobody bewailing today that he was not born in the age of Donizetti. So with the prospect of living in such an age, why do people complain so much?

Workplace Transformation
Respondents explained that in the late 2000s to the current time, more and more companies were exploring the use of models or "bots" to replicate human tasks and undertake more complex financial transactions. The research done in these companies into fostering socially aware digital identities and "bots" aimed to make solutions for the corporate environment simple enough to reach office workers. Several mentioned a vision of excellent Touch Talk Type systems—a vision that was being pursued by a company. A number of mobile applications that exercise AI and machine learning algorithms were gaining traction. They mentioned their growing use for managing emotion in media analytics and trading systems. A parallel development that was significant for them was the increasing number of Algorithmic Business Strategy research papers that helped firms to make decisions closer to the fore of markets that were being remade by the changes taking place.

Over the years, a number of specialists in various industries whom I have spoken with have related the progression of their workplace technology since about the turn of the millennium as a kind of parallel phenomenon. They said that in the late 1990s to around the 2000s, visual and web-based interfaces were introduced that made systems easier to use and faster to learn, laying the groundwork for the rapid diffusion of PCs and Internet access. That allowed companies to enjoy substantial benefits from productivity software and e-commerce. In the early to late 2000s, progress in software engineering techniques enabled complex systems, often run by medium to large organizations, to be built with relatively fewer unsung heroes in software engineering departments. These system architectures could also be altered by change management personnel in response to the needs of business units that utilized them. The business could be well served as long as the underlying rules were not too much in flux.

Human-AI Collaboration

As AI grows in capability and builds upon itself, the day is surely coming when its creators will relinquish control of the AI. At that point, there will be no turning back. Human stewardship will be paramount, for reasons that we have considered earlier. Care for our creations needs to be integral to our AIs, as and when they start to strike out on their own bearings for more parts of their needs. But we will want to aid rather than smother the power of AI that we ourselves have fostered. It will enable us to solve age-old problems, to cope more easily with changes, and to promote understanding and wisdom. In sum, what moraiai suggests is that instead of fearing that we might lose control of our technology, we should concentrate on letting go—such that we might unleash the full potential and capabilities of AI—while never letting go.

Without a goal, AI is rudderless. It needs a human steward. So it turns out that the real problem is not that AI will encroach upon human functioning, but rather that increasingly we will have to explain what really matters to us and figure out how to ask for that from forms of intelligence that matter more to our prospects as a species and as a culture than anything else in the world.

CHAPTER 9

The Ethical and Moral Dimensions of AI

Artificial intelligence is the final and decisive frontier in our knowledge: constructing artificial intelligences is the most powerful instrument in studying our rules (which are very simple because of the invariance principle of our thought) and the ones that are governing the universe. New results to change our view of the world may be posited, to be tested and verified in a context by the scientific community. But who is entitled to trigger these experimentations? And according to which criteria can the results be approved, and to which grade of realization can the obtained results aspire? All the other disciplines are profoundly affected by the potential results, but they neither have the power to activate the experiments that, in fact, are already in place, nor judge the results and choose their degree of realization.

Artificial intelligence (AI) is the final and decisive frontier. It is the modern driver of scientific and social progress and opens up unprecedented possibilities. It can eliminate the heaviest and dirtiest labor and enable humanity to devote itself to higher goals. And yet, it is accompanied by terrifying and unpredictable risks. Workless societies, depersonalization, the formation of a new race with an unequal technological advantage over the rest of humanity, and the impotence of the states against the power of the owners of intelligent machines. Until now, science has always acted by posing hypotheses, carrying out experimental research, and verifying the results. But on top of some given experiments, there used to be an activation barrier beyond which the hypothesis would turn into reality only if public opinion and its representatives agreed to it. Even public opinion is subject to mistakes, but generally, it manages to block unwelcome realities...

Privacy and Surveillance

With practical reasoning and lateral thinking, AI can erode the power of conventional security and civilian privacy protections when it connects multiple sources of data. This poses an inherent risk, from the surveillance state to reduced reproductive freedom, black markets of impeachment, and monopolization of power by a handful of administrations. AI-driven media tools can also distort public policy debates, especially after what is sometimes referred to as the 'synthetic multimedia revolution', i.e. mass manipulation of video and audio footage. This development will make existing debates about the integrity of public officials and electoral campaigns completely academic. Highly credible but manipulated videos of alleged criminal acts or corrupt behavior by public servants or candidates for public office could be used to blackmail, bribe, or frame their targets. "Trust me, I'm real and I could go live any time."

The capability of computer systems to process and analyze data far exceeds the capability of human beings. As this capability increases in sophistication and scope, through both AI as well as more conventional approaches, an increasing portion of all conversations, interactions, and transactions will be fully observable and recorded. As a result, the sensitive information, transactions, and communications can increasingly lead to manipulation, discrimination, and abuse. While encryption, robust identification, and authentication are technological solutions, these will have to be applied in a legal framework that balances security, privacy, and economic interests.

Bias and Discrimination

Fortunately, researchers have started to develop algorithms that can learn in such a way that they make predictions that are less sensitive to undesirable attributes, such as gender and race. Many technical methods are being used to promote fairness and prevent discrimination, such as by choosing which attributes to include or exclude, modifying the training data, and using new and more complex models. Researchers are also increasingly proposing and assessing metrics that can help understand the different impacts and tradeoffs associated with these different algorithmic choices. These efforts are ensuring that a future AI has diverse, equitable, and respectful interactions with all members of the human race.

Bias and discrimination in machine learning have been important topics in the technical literature. The worry is straightforward. Machine learning algorithms are often trained on historical data. That data might not only reflect but embed biases—e.g., biases against women or people of color. If a new machine learning algorithm picks up on these buried prejudices, they might manifest themselves in the algorithm's decisions, choices, and reactions.

Autonomous Weapons

We have noticed that the power that AI represents can be harnessed directly for negative or destructive purposes just as easily as for its numerous positive, constructive uses. As AI's economic, military, social and political impact spreads far and wide, the question is not so much what policy recommendations to pursue to steer the AI revolution in the right direction, but rather how can we take proactive steps to ensure that the direction that the AI revolution takes is well aligned with the long-term best interest of humanity. The alternative is that we allow the power of AI to be dictated by short-term economic, social, and political interests of a small number of important players, and by those so afraid of losing out to new AI capabilities that they will push the establishment of global regulatory constraints on the development and use of strong and effective AI. That is a path we absolutely want to avoid.

We have explored the exciting frontiers of artificial intelligence. We have come to appreciate its potential to solve a wide range of the world's problems. We have also seen the economic, social, and geopolitical implications of the AI revolution. AI is enabling huge new enterprises. It is already enabling new geopolitical constructs to arise and is set to create a new world order that represents a fundamental break with the past.

CHAPTER 10

AI and the Environment

The environmental benefits of energy savings from AI deployment are likely to only be the tip of the iceberg. Machine learning algorithms optimized for better data center management are poised to have an even greater impact than human-manufactured innovations to date. Machine learning can help with huge data center infrastructure tuning, details such as cooling systems or other machinery work together. High computational costs have so far limited this potential. But with fivefold improvements in energy efficiency over the past six years, more improvements in the future, and the operational overhead saved, we can expect machine learning to chip away at these challenges, creating second-order machine learning opportunities. These and similar advances in infrastructure management may offer a roadmap towards a sustainable, high-energy future for people and the environment.

It is not often that technology offers solutions to its own negative externalities. But AI is not like other technologies. AI techniques are making energy grids increasingly efficient. The same is happening with data centers, the factories of AI progress. Microsoft's Tsinghua-Tongfang China data center, for example, uses an advanced, pre-installed cooling system. It saves the local government nearly 500,000 cubic meters of water usage, cuts CO_2 by more than 1000 metric tons, and is 15% more efficient than its local competitors. The energy efficiency program now covers half of Microsoft's data centers and has helped save a cumulative total of 3.4 MWh, enough to power 300,000 US homes for a month.

Climate Change Solutions

Atmospheric carbon capture. Natural solutions are attractive for reducing and offsetting CO_2 emissions, but it seems unlikely we'll be able to meet the growing imbalance between total emissions and natural absorptive capacity with just these techniques (all carbon removal methods combined currently remove less than 1% of the CO_2 emitted by fossil fuel use). And it leads to a new set of opportunities. Lots of these methods also remove particulate pollutants like sulfur dioxide and heavy metals, so the benefits for climate could come faster than the benefits for public health, creating a sort of lose-lose situation where removing carbon creates a temporary spike in warming. However, it may just be worth taking these costs earlier in order to reduce the double damages from particulates. They might even make it much easier to shift into a less carbon-intensive energy economy because these particulate pollutants only linger in the atmosphere for a few weeks, whereas CO_2 lingers for centuries.

Engineered rivers and coastal adaptation. As extreme weather events become more frequent, engineered rivers, which can flexibly change course and take in water, might start making more sense. Coastal cities will need to adapt too, including both reinforcing the coast from storm surges and allowing water in intelligently, as the Dutch are already experimenting with. And the Arctic presents a new set of vulnerabilities. Given the complexity of the climate system and interactions between interventions, it's hard to put specific probabilities on specific events, especially in the near term.

Resource Management

Resource management becomes an even more complex problem for the firm producing an artificial intelligence when one realizes that discoveries about how to make an AI system smarter are nearly always made by the firm that created the AI system in the first place. Traditional improvements to capital equipment occur over time as they diffuse throughout the industry, but not so with super-AIs. The owners of the initial super-AIs have a large lead that cannot be erased by borrowing technology from others. These owners of the most advanced versions of AI tend to have relatively high returns to their investments for a time, which in turn leads to increased industrial concentration as the fastest-learning firms grow bigger faster than do their slower-learning rivals.

Making good use of expensive capital equipment is a central task in any business. In traditional industries, this usually means constructing physical machinery, such as an oil refinery, that meets the needs of the production process. The rapid pace of improvements in information technology products adds an extra wrinkle. A word-processing computer that is cutting-edge today will be inadequate for business needs in four years.

Sustainable Technologies

This generality will come about by developing learning algorithms that can effectively learn from whatever our best code and hardware allow, in those tasks that are relevant to whatever our best human- and machine-generated metrics are. If a system is designed to perform well under one set of conditions and expectations, it will be natural and easy to question whether it has relevance and legitimacy under another set. The only way to protect from obsolescence and exhaustion is to allow and expect continuous learning, evolving as the organization's needs and capacities evolve.

A static answer is almost never an optimal solution for the complex and ever-changing needs of a business. Given the massive improvements in performance experienced by just about every kind of AI system that has ever been benchmarked, it doesn't seem likely that we will run into a roadblock anytime soon. The real bottleneck is that these benchmark improvements do not by themselves change how effectively businesses can apply AI. This necessitates a new generation of learning algorithms that do not require fixed training sets.

CHAPTER 11

The Future of AI Research and Development

At the same time, a multitude of different tasks need to work for technology to be more generally applicable. There are various opinions about the path toward deep theoretical understanding of advanced technologies. Some experts believe it will come only through deliberate self-imposed design constraints, forcing new powerful capabilities to be built on the foundations of a difficult but well-understood starting point. The very success of the early AI projects generated tentative hope that such design constraints might already be visible at the level of choosing rich environments for the collection of data to illustrate results. Such an approach might aid understanding of particular phenomena, but appear to represent too great a compromise for achieving the currently foreseeable potential of human-level generality in AI. The major objection is that such an approach does not deal at all with the possibility of very intelligent entities that may contain remnants of some programmed performers, or even still algorithms.

Thus far, despite significant advantages of an abstractly-specified, capability-control-oriented 'top-down' approach, the field of AI has rather thoroughly explored broad capabilities, in particular building systems that apply a relatively fixed repertoire of human-provided problem-solving methods to a wide range of concrete detailed problems. Thrusting forward into vast new frontiers of generality at the top is probably among the most formidable development tasks in the field's history. AI research today is in an unusual position as a field of science. It has been producing systems that can do demonstrations of superhuman ability, but has barely begun to understand the underlying phenomena, because understanding occurred after the ability existed. Researchers who actually design and deploy systems that do a wide variety of difficult-to-describe tasks do not yet have a well-defined highly leveraged path to move their local knowledge into generality.

Advances in Machine Learning

Subsection Title: A Brief History of Machine Learning One of the major reasons we have chosen to organize this chapter around a general AI timeline is to give readers a chance to reflect on the broader AI-related themes. They will be overwhelmed with the countless AI developments that have taken place over the years. It would be highly impractical to attempt to track all machine learning-related events back to their historical roots, so we have opted for a brief timeline starting in 1950. The interested reader may refer to Gentle, Machine Learning Yearning, and other focused material for guidance. The primary reason we make this two-tier list is that there are a few seminal developments that we believe are more likely to catch the interest of a broader audience. Not the least because readers may have encountered historical references to some of these developments in lectures, seminars, readings, and discussions with colleagues. We hope that in return for this omission, we will have provided our readers a broad, yet valuable, short overview on the growth of machine learning (where we also include substantial contributions from disciplines lying at the frontier between ML and related fields such as Control).

One of the new topics we introduced this year included a section with a general timeline of machine learning-related developments. As it is often the case, a timeline naturally offers more space for some events, to the detriment of others. We are more than aware that the timeline we present in this section leaves out a wealth of important AI-related developments, but we sincerely hope the selected events can provide valuable guidance to the casually interested reader. Furthermore, the short time devoted to each event can also serve as a reference point for the depth of detail presented in the subsequent sections. Providing such a timeline is a challenging endeavor, and we apologize in advance to the colleagues we may have overlooked.

Neural Networks and Deep Learning

The first term to focus on to understand what a feedforward or multilayer perceptron neural network describes is that of approximator. The approximation of a scalar function can be understood quite well in two or three dimensions; but from three dimensions onwards, the representation becomes complex. The learning problem can, after all, be mapped onto a memorization problem (a search for memorization or learning events that generalize well to training data in bearings that are ultimately spaced by the desired outputs), albeit possibly in a particular function space; but in the latter case, these functions belong to a priori favored functional spaces. Further, additional problems derive from the fact that these a priori motivations must allow the emergence of feedback architectures and may depend on the chosen cost function and the adopted training. The hierarchical organization of the functions is such that the function returned at an intermediate level depends and progressively refines the features captured at lower levels.

If the history of neural networks were a textbook example of an exponential-accelerating development, it would be evident that the neural network approach, which is essentially a machine learning approach, could generate increasingly efficient and innovative systems. Indeed, for mastering a particular task, as we saw in the previous chapter, even with neural networks we need well-designed ML systems, which take into account the task itself, the type of training data, etc. (provided powerful deep learning systems that are both efficient and innovative against those that are neither), it is necessary to feed in a slightly more intuitive idea that links ML and its variation: neural networks. The main idea is to make explicit the functional complexity inherent in many real-world problems and, thus, to understand how deep or complex or intelligent learning systems make the problem's modeling process through parametric functions.

Deep learning is that type of artificial intelligence that has caused so much enthusiasm in the meantime and for good reasons. It refers to systems composed of large-scale neural networks, typically with millions or even billions of parameters. Neural networks have been known for a long time, but there was a time when the results were poor. The reason, we know today, is that those networks were simple. But with years of research and especially with the enormous increase in the size of data sets and improvement in training algorithms, the performance improved exponentially. Consequently, the interests of the research and industrial community in neural networks followed the same ever-increasing trend. Today, billions of dollars are invested in neural network technology and their applications. Companies that for many years have been focused on image and video recognition, speech recognition, and AI are immensely wealthy. The one that brought deep learning to the forefront-work-ing on all but the first one of these applications-was Baidu, the Chinese search engine company, which established a strong research and development center in California to take advantage of the United States' favorable research environment.

AI Ethics and Governance

Whatever intuition we have about how the world will look after machines replace people in most physical labor should apply to the year when such machines replace people in most cognitive and creative labor instead. Work is useful to society only insofar as other people care about the outcome. The distribution of the benefits of this kind of work will be as divisive as any other change in technology, and the nature of what people are good for will change as dramatically as have their muscles. We can use the same economic and political instruments that we have used to smooth out previous transitions of this kind. But we need to use them with care because the age of creative, intelligent machines is so different.

We think that the main benefits of this revolution are obvious. Having machines that are better than humans at thinking, at least in some very important ways, will make our lives much better. But while the main benefits of the AI revolution are obvious, they will not necessarily come automatically. We have to educate our kids not just about history and physics and a lot of other little things, but also about the tools that they can use to ride the AI wave. Yes, very few of them will become inventors or even developers of these new technologies, just as very few of them will become historians or physicists. But centuries of experience with science and math show that even future citizens who never managed to learn them in depth get lots of benefits just from being close enough to smell them.

CHAPTER 12

Conclusion and Looking Ahead

In this book, we've discussed the rise of artificial intelligence in detail. We saw that AI has been convincingly beating humans at a number of narrow tasks, and that AI progresses on many of these narrower tasks has been gradually converging in practice (known as "encompassing" in AI races). In the short to medium run, we expect the rise of AI to continue — more encompassing progress and still quite a bit of AI surprises to be had. Whether we've really reached human-level performance or have merely created specialized systems that achieve human-level results within their respective niches, an age of general AI — superintelligent machines — is on the horizon.

Looking ahead, one of the central paradoxes of the AI age is that while so many people are talking about general AI as the destination, not many people seem to be talking about intelligence as the journey. The journey may be very long. Because, it isn't just about building a machine that can do the things that a human can, but 1,000x better in every conceivable way, but repeatedly doing so for every product on the market, just as humans have done for thousands of years in order to build the world around us. The destination may very well recede, as the journey will likely reveal abilities that we are both good at and that we prize. Because of this, we should be committed to both being here today and pushing the AI frontier forward. The long journey is something for the serious traveler, and we're only in the early stages of a very long trip. However, the long journey is something for the serious traveler, and we're only in the early stages of a very long trip. The Renaissance served as a rich pool that spawned the industrial revolution because the society produced together an infrastructure that fired, and as a result we created the politics of administration. Hopefully, with the increasing globalization of AI progress, we will be able to do the same with artificial intelligence. Then, the age of AI will be as much an age of joy and prosperity as it is an age of inspiration and invention.